THE ART OF WRESTLING

THE

Art *of* Wrestling

By

G. DE RELWYSKOW

LIGHT-WEIGHT CHAMPION OF THE WORLD
ALSO WINNER OF WORLD'S CHAMPIONSHIP
FOR GREAT BRITAIN AT THE GREAT
OLYMPIC GAMES.

The Naval & Military Press Ltd

Published by

The Naval & Military Press Ltd
Unit 5 Riverside, Brambleside
Bellbrook Industrial Estate
Uckfield, East Sussex
TN22 1QQ England

Tel: +44 (0)1825 749494

www.naval-military-press.com
www.nmarchive.com

FOREWORD

MR. DE RELWYSKOW, late of the Army Gymnastic Staff, has asked me for a foreword. I am only too pleased to do this for him.

He was employed, as principal Wrestling Instructor on the Army Gymnastic Staff, in France and England for over two years, during which time he worked loyally and with untiring energy. Not only does he thoroughly understand his work, but he has the brain and imagination to understand the difficulties of a beginner. He understands the art of teaching.

His methods of instruction produced excellent results. He made his pupils like their work; he seemed to inspire them with the Spirit of Wrestling and clean sport. I am pleased he has written a book. It will be of great value in teaching the science of Wrestling on the right lines, and perhaps be the means of reviving the interest in it.

I wish his effort every possible success.

R. B. CAMPBELL,

Colonel,

Inspector of Physical Training.

HEADQUARTERS, P.T.,

ALDERSHOT.

10*th June,* 1919.

AN APPRECIATION

Captain Daniels, V.C., M.C., Rifle Brigade, states:—

"In adding a word to this book on the style of wrestling as taught at the Headquarters Gymnasium of the British Army, and having had personal experience in the various holds and throws taught, I consider it has been of great value in the training of the soldier, and the bringing out of those qualities of grit and determination which have been seen in all ranks who have taken an active part throughout the greatest war in history."

H. Daniels,
Captain.

1919.

AUTHOR'S PREFACE

WRESTLING can well be claimed as perhaps the oldest competitive sport known to mankind. It has flourished in all ages and among all nations, by its appeals to the manhood of a people in a way that no other sport has or ever can. It arises from man's natural instinct to overcome an opponent by sheer physical skill and strength with the aid of nature's only weapons—hands, arms, feet, and legs. Wrestling has become a science that has many attractions to the athlete. I devoted many years to the study of the science and have evolved a system based on the principle of preserving balance that will be found of some value to all who take up wrestling in any of its styles, and will, moreover, be found of great assistance to all as a very effective and easily mastered form of self-defence.

G. DE RELWYSKOW,
Light-weight Champion of the World.

LONDON,
1924.

PUBLISHERS' ANNOUNCEMENT

How well qualified Mr. G. de Relwyskow is to teach wrestling his record will show. He is an Englishman of Russian descent, and was selected to represent Great Britain as a wrestler at the Olympic Games in London in 1908, where he won the World's Light-Weight Championship in the Catch-as-Catch-Can style. An artist and designer by profession, he took up wrestling as an athletic exercise and hobby during his student days in London. He became so proficient that as an amateur he won the championship of Great Britain four times—twice as a light-weight, and twice as a middle-weight—giving away a stone and a half each time in the latter event. He won over fifty open competitions in England before competing in the Olympic Games.

After winning the World's Amateur Championship he took up wrestling as a profession, meeting and defeating most of the famous wrestlers, among them Peter Gotz, for the Professional Light-Weight Championship of the World. He had never been defeated when the Great War broke out. He was then touring South America, but took the earliest opportunity of returning to England and enlisting. He was posted to the Army Gymnastic Staff, and for a time was attached to the Australian Infantry as an instructor in physical training and bayonet fighting. Proceeding to France, he rendered good service by introducing a system of hand-to-hand fighting and wrestling for the use of patrols and raiders. This he taught to classes of unit instructors, who in turn trained selected men in all the battalions on the Western Front for this special duty.

Returning to England in October, 1918, he was posted to the Headquarters Gymnasium, Aldershot, as an instructor in the Army system of wrestling, which was invented by him and accepted as the official style for the Army, the principles of which are embodied in these pages.

CONTENTS

	PAGE
INTRODUCTORY	1
WRESTLING ON THE FEET	3
TIPS FOR THE BEGINNER	5
TIPS FOR INSTRUCTORS	7
SUGGESTED COURSE OF HALF-HOUR LESSONS	7
FIRST LESSON	7
SECOND LESSON	8
THIRD LESSON	9
FOURTH LESSON	9
STANDARD WEIGHTS	10
RULES OF WRESTLING ON THE FEET	10
SIMPLE COMPETITIONS	12
WRESTLING MATS	13

LIST OF PLATES

THE AUTHOR ... ... *Frontispiece*

PLATE   PAGE

I. POSITION OF BODY 15
II. INITIAL HOLD 16
III. CROSS-BUTTOCK (*Position* 1) 19
IV. CROSS-BUTTOCK (*Position* 2) 19
V. CROSS-BUTTOCK (*Position* 3) 19
VI. CROSS-BUTTOCK, USING THE LEG 20
VII. STOP FOR CROSS-BUTTOCK 20
VIII. WAIST-BUTTOCK 23
IX. WAIST-BUTTOCK—*continued* 23
X. WAIST-BUTTOCK—*continued* 23
XI. STOP FOR WAIST-BUTTOCK 24
XII. STOP AND COUNTER TO WAIST-BUTTOCK ... 24
XIII. ARM-THROW (*Position* 1) 27
XIV. ARM-THROW (*Position* 2) 27
XV. ARM-THROW AND GRAPE-VINE 28
XVI. COUNTER TO CROSS-BUTTOCK AND DOUBLE
(*Position* 1) 31
XVII. COUNTER TO CROSS-BUTTOCK AND DOUBLE
(*Position* 2) 31
XVIII. COUNTER TO CROSS-BUTTOCK AND DOUBLE
(*Position* 3) 31
XIX. STOP AND COUNTER TO WAIST-HOLD FROM
BEHIND 32
XX. FLYING MARE (*Position* 1) 35
XXI. FLYING MARE (*Position* 2) 35
XXII. GRAPE-VINE AND WAIST-THROW 36
XXIII. STOP AND COUNTER FOR THE FLYING MARE
(*Position* 1) 39
XXIV. STOP AND COUNTER FOR THE FLYING MARE
(*Position* 2) 39
XXV. HALF-HALCH 40
XXVI. THE HALCH 40
XXVII. STOP FOR HALF-HALCH OR HALCH 40
XXVIII. DOUBLE-ARM THROW FROM UNDERNEATH
(*Position* 1) 43
XXIX. DOUBLE-ARM THROW FROM UNDERNEATH
(*Position* 2) 43
XXX. THE HANK (*Position* 1) 44
XXXI. THE HANK (*Position* 2) 44
XXXII. BACK-HEEL (OUT OF DISTANCE) 47
XXXIII. LEG-THROW (IN GRIPS) (*Position* 1) 48

PLATE		PAGE
XXXIV.	Leg-Throw (in Grips) (*Position 2*)	48
XXXV.	Waist-Hold and Back-Heel	51
XXXVI.	Stop and Counter for Waist-Hold ...	52
XXXVII.	Outside Stroke	55
XXXVIII.	To get Behind Opponent out of Distance	55
XXXIX.	To get Behind Opponent in Grips ...	56
XL.	Throw from Behind	56
XLI.	Throw from Behind	59
XLII.	Throw from Behind	59
XLIII.	Throw from Behind	59
XLIV.	Half-Nelson and Waist-Hold from Behind	60
XLV.	Counter to Waist-Hold from Behind (*Position 1*)	63
XLVI.	Counter to Waist-Hold from Behind (*Position 2*)	63
XLVII.	Hammer Lock and Back-Heel	64
XLVIII.	Stop to Hammer Lock	64
XLIX.	Full Nelson	67
L.	Butcher's Hook Grip	68
LI.	Single Wrist Grip	68
LII.	Double Wrist Grip	68
LIII.	Interlacing Fingers	68
LIV.	First Leg Exercise	71
LV.	Second Leg Exercise	71
LVI.	Neck Exercise	72
LVII.	Leg and Back Exercises	75
LVIII.	Leg and Back Exercises	75
LIX.	Arm Exercise	76
LX.	Trunk and Leg Exercises	76
LXI.	Self-Defence for Women	79
LXII.	Self-Defence for Women	79
LXIII.	Self-Defence for Women	79

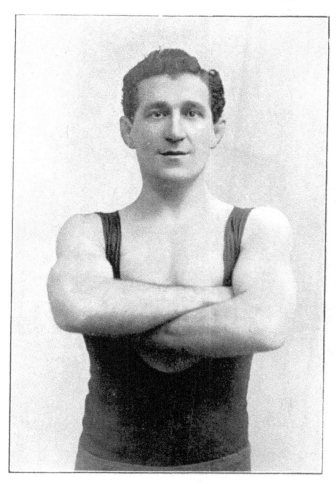

THE AUTHOR.

WRESTLING

INTRODUCTORY

WRESTLING is one of the oldest forms of athletics, and has always strongly appealed to the British because of its competitive sporting spirit, aroused by the cultivation of its manly attributes of strength, agility, physical endurance, and good temper. These attributes are necessary on the part of those who desire to become experts in the art. Wrestling in some form or other was practised by nearly all the ancient nations, but the rules varied considerably. In some cases a victory was achieved when an opponent was thrown to the ground from a standing position; while in others, where brute strength was the dominant factor, an opponent was only considered defeated when he was so injured or in such a state of exhaustion that he could no longer continue the contest. In these rough encounters death or very extensive and permanent injuries were not infrequent. Such was the nature of the old Roman wrestling matches, and there is every reason to believe that the Romans introduced this form of athletic contest into England after they had successfully invaded these islands. The Romans left, but wrestling remained in England, and was practised according to varying rules in different parts of the country. It continued to be a very rough kind of sport for hundreds of years, but gradually brains as well as brawn was needed to become a champion, until now the art is founded and taught on scientific principles.

Before the Great War the military value of wrestling had not been seriously considered or studied, chiefly because of the want of uniformity of rules then prevailing. But when the opposing armies in France and Flanders settled down to trench warfare the advantage of wrestling as an invaluable aid in the grim hand-to-hand struggles that marked the nightly raids was soon recognized. Then it was that wrestling began to be systematically taught and practised by the British Army on the Western Front, and this form of athletics has now become firmly established in favour not only among all ranks of the Army but also in civilian sporting circles. This is undoubtedly due to our simplified form of wrestling which, while affording a valuable means of military training, also appeals to men of all grades of physical development. It has a definite military training value, is competitive, and, like boxing, can be made to foster the team spirit.

This important style of wrestling is based on the principle of maintaining balance on the feet, for as soon as any part of the head, body, hands, or limbs, with the exception of the soles of the feet, touch the floor, a point is scored. As a physical exercise this form of wrestling calls for agility, endurance, quick judgment, and good temper. It is the most natural method of overcoming an opponent when in close grips, and the most practical to use as a means of self-defence in the event of being attacked from behind or in front by a footpad. By this system of wrestling an assailant's own violence can be utilized to overcome him by applying one or other of the "throws" demonstrated in this book.

The study of this style of wrestling will prove a sound foundation on which to build a knowledge of other styles, for it trains a wrestler to keep his feet, and to quickly recover balance when nearly thrown by an opponent.

It is also of considerable value to boxers, for it teaches how best to use one's weight and conserve one's strength when in clutches.

WRESTLING ON THE FEET.

Wrestlers in the past, in my opinion, have given far too much of their time in struggling on the mat, and have not paid sufficient attention to the most important part : that is, how to maintain their balance when coming to grips with a much stronger opponent. Therefore men who had a good knowledge of wrestling on the ground have been thrown off their feet by an inferior wrestler simply because they had not studied the most essential part of wrestling —leverage and balance. I have therefore embodied in this book locks, throws, trips and counters, which, I am sure, amateurs and professionals will appreciate. Furthermore, I have arranged a system of lessons by means of which instructors of schools or classes, small or large, will be able to show satisfactory results.

I have also arranged a system of competitions or contests which men who are beginners can take part in, and by means of which the most essential part in all games, the competitive spirit, is introduced and fostered.

In nearly all the throws in this book, if you maintain your hold on your opponent you will be able to secure a pin fall on him without any wrestling on the mat, so you can see the advantage of being a good wrestler on your feet; in fact, when you have mastered wrestling on your feet, and should you decide to specialize in any other style of wrestling where it is necessary to get your opponent to the mat and continue wrestling for a fall, you will be able to gain the master position immediately by bringing off one of the trips or throws illustrated in this book.

The introduction of this style of wrestling into the British Army was eminently successful, being simple to teach, attractive to learn, and, when used as a competitive athletic exercise, easy to judge. The rules are few and simple, and beyond the ordinary gymnasium mats for indoor work no apparatus is needed. As showing how quickly the principles of this style of wrestling are mastered, I once refereed a competition in the 50th Division which lasted two days, so numerous were the competitors, the great majority of whom had known nothing whatever about this or any other style of wrestling before being taken in hand by the Army Gymnastic Staff Instructor a month previously.

I experienced the same sort of thing in many other units where I refereed or gave demonstrations. I also found that in many of the convalescent camps in France this style of wrestling had been adopted as a form of physical and recreational training, and was taken up with enthusiasm by the patients.

TIPS FOR THE BEGINNER.

First learn how to fall. This can be done by falling about on the mat or grass, first by yourself, and then by getting a comrade to practise with you. Allow him to Cross-buttock you and trip you, and put the Flying Mare on you, then in time you will be able to take a fall with ease and without hurting yourself.

Always take care to fall limp, with muscles relaxed. Comparatively few drunken people hurt themselves when they fall, due to the fact that they do not attempt to break the fall by bracing the limbs or muscles.

Being able to fall easily and without injury is a great advantage to a wrestler.

When you find your opponent has a good hold on you, and you can't prevent him throwing you, don't hang on to him, for you will only get his weight on top of you, and this may knock all the fight out of you for the next bout. Therefore, when you realize you can't stop an opponent throwing you, try to loosen out and fall clear of him.

In learning or practising always try to get an opponent a little heavier than yourself. This will prove an advantage to you when you wrestle with a man at or under your own weight.

When wrestling always keep cool, keep your wits about you, and never lose your temper. As soon as a man loses his temper when wrestling he sends a signal to his opponent that something is wrong. This will give his opponent renewed confidence, although he may have been losing heart; he will make renewed efforts, and perhaps win.

When you are wrestling don't grip your opponent unnecessarily tight, as it only tires your arms. Don't grip tight until you get the hold you are after. When you have got the position you want, use all your reserve strength and try to accomplish your throw.

Don't let your opponent see what hold you are after, for it gives him a chance to get ready, and so stop or counter you. Try and deceive him as to your intentions till you see the opening you want, then slip in quickly and surprise him, using all your strength.

If your opponent is thick-set and has big muscles don't be afraid of him. Such men are frequently the easiest to beat, because they are generally slow in movement.

Don't forget that brain work is needed in wrestling as well as muscles and weight, so don't trust to your strength alone.

TIPS FOR INSTRUCTORS.

Form your class in two ranks; quickly pair front and rear rank men off, so that each pair are about the same age, weight, physique, and as near as possible of the same temperament.

For the second and subsequent lessons change partners, so that the same pair are not always wrestling together.

Always commence and finish the lesson with bouts of wrestling.

Arouse the competitive spirit in your class by getting one man to challenge another to a bout on the mat.

Engender good temper and feeling by making the men shake hands before and after wrestling.

Promptly check any tendency to foul play.

SUGGESTED COURSE OF HALF-HOUR LESSONS.

FIRST LESSON.

Get your class round you, and give them a lecture lasting three or four minutes on the usefulness of wrestling as a form of self-defence, the military style, and the principles and rules of the game.

Pick out one of the class and get him to try to wrestle you. Pull each other about without throwing, lasting about one minute.

Now fall you class in, size off, etc.; then give the command "For Wrestling Practice— Move." The front rank will turn about and pair off with rear rank, and immediately extend out. Shake hands, and commence wrestling—pulling each other about without actually trying to throw.

Now that the class have had a feeler, and have got an idea of how to keep their balance, call them round you and teach position of body for attack and defence. (Plate 1.)

Class practise this position moving about without coming to grips.

Teach initial hold (Plate 2), and get class to practise same.

Teach the Cross-buttock, and let class practise on the mat or grass. (Plates 3, 4, and 5.)

Finish First Lesson by wrestling bouts without throwing. This is to inculcate good and quick movement of the body and preserving balance.

Second Lesson.

Commence with bouts of wrestling without throws, as in First Lesson.

Teach Stop for Cross-buttock. (Plate 7.) Allow class to practise.

8

Teach Waist-buttock. (Plate 8.) **Allow** class to practise and throw each other. (Instructor correcting faults.)

Teach Stop for Waist-buttock. (Plate 11.) Allow class to practise.

Teach Counter to Cross-buttock and Double. (Plates 16, 17, and 18.) Bring class out in pairs, and get them to wrestle a bout, trying for a throw. Instructor refereeing.

End of Second Lesson.

THIRD LESSON.

Commence with wrestling bouts, men trying for a throw.

Teach Flying Mare. (Plates 20 and 21.) Instructor should stand close up to men practising this to catch man being thrown, in order to instil confidence.

Teach Stop and Counter for Flying Mare. (Plate 23.) Allow class to practise.

Teach Back-Heel Out of Distance. (Plate 32.) Instructor must take care to see that the man tripped does not purposely fall.

Teach Leg Throw in Grips. (Plates 33 and 34.) Complete lesson with bouts of wrestling, men trying for throws.

End of Third Lesson.

FOURTH LESSON.

Commence lesson with bouts of wrestling, men trying for throws.

9

Teach men how to get behind opponent out of distance. (Plates 17, 18, and 38.) Allow class to practise to right and left.

Teach men how to get behind opponent when in grips. (Plate 39.) Allow class to practise.

Teach men how to throw from behind. (Plates 40, 41, 42, and 43.) Allow class to practise, and finish them with wrestling bouts.

If subsequent lessons are possible, the Instructor can teach other throws, as shown in this book, giving plenty of practice in individual bouts. Class competitions can also be arranged for instructional and practice purposes.

STANDARD WEIGHTS OF THE NATIONAL AMATEUR WRESTLING ASSOCIATION AND OLYMPIC GAMES

123lbs.—Bantam-weights.
134lbs.—Feather-weights.
145lbs.—Light-weights.
158lbs.—Welter-weights.
174lbs.—Middle-weights.
191lbs.—Light Heavy-weights.
Heavy-weights, Catch-weights.

THE RULES FOR WRESTLING ON THE FEET.

In organizing competitions for wrestling on the feet, the following rules must be adhered to :—

A Flying Fall is gained when a man's shoulders touch the ground simultaneously.

In Catch-as-Catch-Can Wrestling the competitor can take hold above or below the waist excepting vulnerable parts of the body; also the Strangle Hold and Full Nelson is barred.

A Pin Fall in Catch-as-Catch-Can style is gained when a man's two shoulders are held to the ground for two seconds.

The wrestlers may take hold anywhere above the legs, subject to the following restrictions :—
The hair, flesh, ears, and clothing may not be seized; butting with the head or shoulder and twisting of fingers or thumbs are forbidden; nor shall any hold be allowed which threatens the breakage or dislocation of a limb, and which may induce the wrestler so held to concede the fall. Kicking is forbidden, but striking with the side of the foot or the sole of the foot shall not be termed kicking.

A "fall" shall be allotted to a wrestler when his opponent touches the ground with any part of his body other than his feet. Although the latter may still retain his hold, he shall not be allowed to continue the bout, but shall be adjudged the loser.

If both wrestlers fall to the ground, the man who is first down or who is undermost shall be the loser. If they fall simultaneously side by side, or in any other fashion that prevents the judges from deciding which was first down, the fall shall be called a "Dog Fall," and shall have no value for either man, and they will get up and wrestle on.

The wrestlers shall compete in stockinged feet and wear rubber-soled gymnasium shoes.

At every contest or competition there shall be not fewer than two judges, who shall arbitrate with the referee. The decision of one judge alone shall not be accepted, and the referee, when the judges are not unanimous, shall decide. The referee shall have power also to decide any point not provided for by these rules.

The referee shall immediately disqualify any man using unfair or illegal methods.

SIMPLE COMPETITIONS.

The following are methods by which class competitions are easily arranged for recreational training :—

1. The class is formed into a circle, each man being allowed to select his own opponent.

2. Front Rank v. Rear Rank. Both ranks having been sized off, are faced inwards, wrestling space being left between the ranks. Starting from the right of the class, the winner of each bout takes the loser back to his rank with him. The rank having the largest number at the completion of the bouts wins.

WRESTLING MATS.

1. Six or twelve gymnasium mats laid together, so as to form a square, and a canvas cover or carpet laid over the top, make an ideal mat.

2. Make a wooden frame 16 or 20 feet square, fill in with sawdust or peat about 4 inches higher than the frame, then nail some canvas over the top. This makes a very good mat.

3. Get sixty flour sacks and fill them with straw or hay, then sew them together. Sew the sacks about 3 inches above the side seam, and pull tightly together.

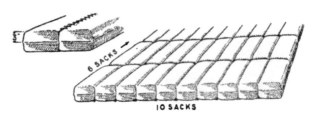

6 SACKS

10 SACKS

4. A nice grass plot makes the best mat of all, and costs nothing.

Plate I.

POSITION OF BODY FOR ATTACK OR DEFENCE.

(*Note.*—Feet fairly well apart ; knees slightly bent ; body forward ; prepared to lay whole weight on opponent immediately on coming to grips ; hands advanced, one slightly in front of other ; eyes on opponent. If moving to the right, move right foot outwards first, followed by left foot. If to the left, reverse the movement. Carefully avoid crossing the feet, as this gives your opponent a chance of catching you off your balance.)

PLATE I.

PLATE II.

PLATE II.

INITIAL HOLD.

Right hand round neck ; left hand on upper arm
just above elbow ; weight of body resting on
opponent to prevent opponent applying the
cross-buttock.

(*Note.*—Referee may order men to take this position should they occupy too much time in
sparring for an opening.)

17

PLATE III.

CROSS-BUTTOCK (*Position* 1).

Seize opponent's right elbow with left hand ; slip
right arm round neck as in initial hold.

PLATE IV.

CROSS-BUTTOCK (*Position* 2).

Retaining hold, bring right hip sharply under
opponent, and turn body completely round,
at the same time slightly bending knees ;
feet well apart.

PLATE V.

CROSS-BUTTOCK (*Position* 3).

By a quick, vigorous straightening of the knees,
a strong downward pull of the right arm,
and a heave of the left shoulder, throw
opponent.

(*Note.*—Should opponent hang on, fall on him.
This will help to lessen his resistance in the
next bout.)

PLATE III.

PLATE IV.

PLATE V.

19

PLATE VII.

PLATE VI.

29

PLATE VI.

CROSS-BUTTOCK, USING THE LEG.

If opponent drops back to avoid the cross-buttock,
quickly strike the outside of his right leg with
your right, at the same time pulling him over
with the cross-buttock.

PLATE VII.

STOP FOR CROSS-BUTTOCK.

As opponent tries to turn in for cross-buttock,
quickly push your left forearm out across
his ribs. The left hand can be used in same
manner.

PLATE VIII.

WAIST-BUTTOCK.

Exactly the same as cross-buttock, except that
right arm is placed around opponent's waist
instead of neck.

PLATE IX.

WAIST-BUTTOCK—*continued*.

If opponent hangs back, throw yourself forward,
head over heels. This will bring opponent
underneath on ground.

PLATE X.

WAIST-BUTTOCK—*continued*.

Throw completed.

PLATE IX.

PLATE X.

PLATE VIII.

23

PLATE XII.

PLATE XI.

24

PLATE XI.

STOP FOR WAIST-BUTTOCK.

As opponent turns in, place left hand quickly
under his right jaw and push him away.

PLATE XII.

STOP AND COUNTER TO WAIST-
BUTTOCK.

Before opponent can recover from the stop, slip
right hip behind his and throw him with a
hip-buttock.

Plate XIII.

ARM-THROW (*Position* 1).

When attempting a cross-buttock and opponent drops his head to avoid your right arm.

Plate XIV.

ARM-THROW (*Position* 2).

Quickly step in, grip his right arm with both hands, turn body round, as in cross-buttock, and throw him over your hip.

PLATE XIII.

PLATE XIV.

PLATE XV.

PLATE XV.

ARM-THROW AND GRAPE-VINE.

When in position for arm-throw and opponent
hangs back, entwine your right leg around
his right leg ; quickly straighten your leg out,
and pull him over. This movement with the
leg is known as the grape-vine.

PLATE XVI.

COUNTER TO CROSS-BUTTOCK AND DOUBLE (*Position* 1).

As opponent turns in for the cross-buttock, sharply push his right arm over your head with your left hand, and swing him round ; at the same time step behind him.

PLATE XVII.

COUNTER TO CROSS-BUTTOCK AND DOUBLE (*Position* 2).

Transfer left arm round opponent's waist, and clasp your own wrist. Bending your knees, pull opponent in tightly to your waist ; straighten your legs out and lift him.

PLATE XVIII.

COUNTER TO CROSS-BUTTOCK AND DOUBLE (*Position* 3).

Now swing opponent off his balance and throw him.

PLATE XVIII.

PLATE XVII.

PLATE XVI.

31

PLATE XIX.

32

PLATE XIX.

STOP AND COUNTER TO WAIST-HOLD FROM BEHIND.

Entwine your legs round your opponent's, inside
or outside.   Keep in this position until he tires
and attempts to release his hold.   As soon
as he drops you, cross-buttock him as in
Plates 5, 6 and 7.

33

Plate XX.

FLYING MARE (*Position* 1).

Seize opponent's right arm with left hand, and turn quickly in front of him; slip right shoulder under his right armpit, at the same time seizing his right upper arm with both hands.

Plate XXI.

FLYING MARE (*Position* 2).

Give a vigorous pull forward, at the same time straightening your legs, and bring opponent over your shoulder.

(*Note.*—When practising this throw, opponent should lay his head on your left shoulder and you should hold on to his right arm as long as possible. This will prevent opponent striking the ground with his head.)

PLATE XXI.

PLATE XX.

35

PLATE XXII.

PLATE XXII.

GRAPE-VINE AND WAIST-THROW.

If opponent stops you turning into the Flying
Mare, slip right arm round his back and apply
the Grape-Vine with your right leg. Now
quickly straighten your leg and pull him
over.

PLATE XXIII.

STOP AND COUNTER FOR THE FLYING MARE (*Position* 1).

When opponent secures position for the Flying Mare, press your left hand in the small of his back, and press on his right leg with your right knee.

PLATE XXIV.

STOP AND COUNTER FOR THE FLYING MARE (*Position* 2).

Then quickly step forward and place right hip in the small of his back. Straighten legs and throw him over your waist.

38

PLATE XXIV.

PLATE XXIII.

39

PLATE XXVII.

PLATE XXVI.

PLATE XXV.

PLATE XXV.

HALF-HALCH.

Pull opponent in to you from initial hold (Plate 23).
Slip left arm under his right arm, his head
under your right arm. From this position
swing your opponent over to your right.
(This throw can be made to the left by
reversing the arms.)

PLATE XXVI.

THE HALCH.

Pull opponent in, slipping both arms under his and
around his back. Lock your hands and swing
to right or left until he is off his balance,
then throw.

PLATE XXVII.

STOP FOR HALF-HALCH OR HALCH.

Place your free hand on opponent's hip and force
him away. One or both hands can be used
as a stop for the Full-Halch.

PLATE XXVIII.

DOUBLE-ARM THROW FROM UNDER-NEATH (*Position* 1).

Seize opponent's wrists, backs of your hands inwards, slip your head and shoulders under him, lock his elbows to your sides, still retaining hold of wrists.

PLATE XXIX.

DOUBLE-ARM THROW FROM UNDER-NEATH (*Position* 2).

Straighten legs smartly, lift, and throw him over your back. If he hangs on to you, fall on him.

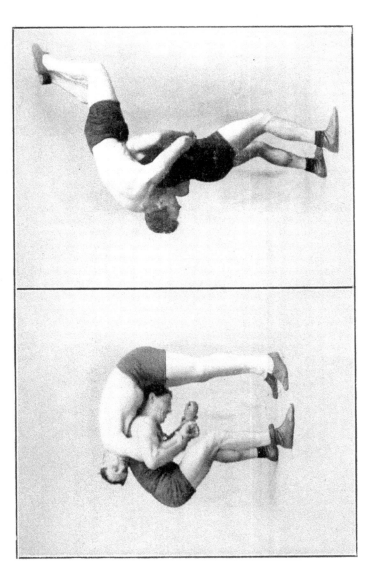

PLATE XXVIII.

PLATE XXIX.

61

PLATE XXX.

PLATE XXXI.

PLATE XXX.

THE HANK (*Position* 1).

Pretend to turn in for cross-buttock, but instead
slip right leg around his left.

PLATE XXXI.

THE HANK (*Position* 2).

Fall backwards, straightening right leg, and pull
opponent to the ground under you.

(*Note.*—The Hank can often be used as a counter
when an opponent has hold of you from
behind.)

PLATE XXXII.

BACK-HEEL (OUT OF DISTANCE).

If opponent approaches with left leg forward, step
quickly in and strike behind his left leg with
your left leg. This must be done quickly
with the weight of your body forward. The
same can be done right leg against right leg.

PLATE XXXII.

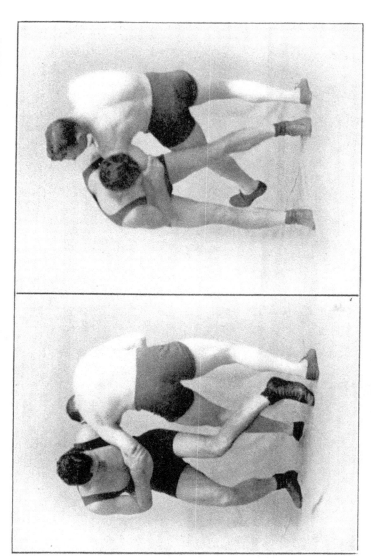

PLATE XXXIV.

PLATE XXXIII.

Plate XXXIII.

LEG THROW (IN GRIPS)
(*Position* 1).

When in grips and opponent has left leg forward,
quickly slip left leg with bent knee behind
his, keeping weight of your body forward.

Plate XXXIV.

LEG THROW (IN GRIPS)
(*Position* 2).

Sharply straighten left leg, striking him behind
the hock with inside of knee. This can be
done with right leg.

PLATE XXXV.

WAIST-HOLD AND BACK-HEEL.

Slip inside opponent's guard, place arms round
waist, and grip your wrists ; pull him in
tight, place one of your heels behind his,
and throw.

Plate XXXV.

PLATE XXXVI.

PLATE XXXVI.

STOP AND COUNTER FOR WAIST-HOLD.

Thrust opponent's head away with your hands under his jaw. Having broken his hold, counter by cross-buttock (Plates 5, 6, and 7).

Plate XXXVII.

OUTSIDE STROKE.

As opponent steps forward, before he can transfer
his weight to the forward foot, strike on the
outside with the sole of your opposite foot, at
the same time pulling him off his balance.

Plate XXXVIII.

TO GET BEHIND OPPONENT OUT OF DISTANCE.

When approaching to get into grips, seize opponent's left elbow with left hand, and with
a sharp semi-circular pull swing him round.
Then, jumping behind him, grip him around
the waist, and swing and throw (Plates 17
and 18).

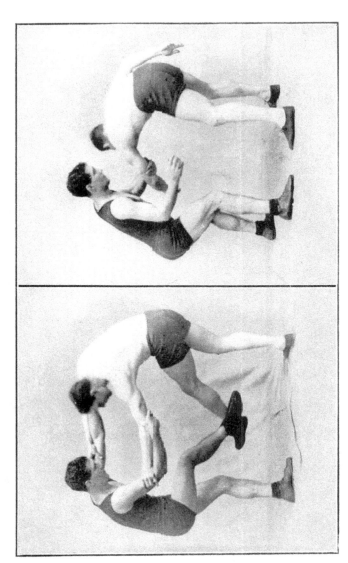

PLATE XXXVII.

PLATE XXXVIII.

55

PLATE XL.

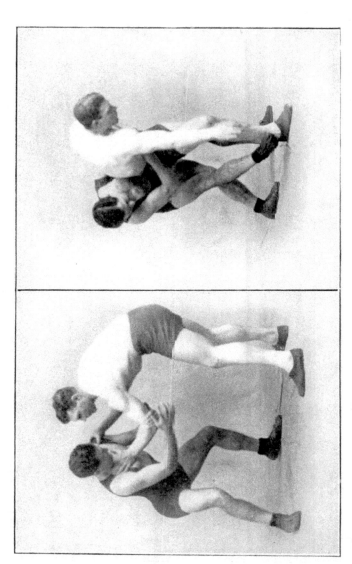

PLATE XXXIX.

PLATE XXXIX.

TO GET BEHIND OPPONENT IN GRIPS.

Take opponent's left elbow or arm with both hands,
and pull in the same manner.   Opponent can
be swung to left or right by reversing the
hands.

To counter, place left hand on opponent's chest
or under jaw and thrust him away as he
attempts to swing.

PLATE XL.

THROW FROM BEHIND.

Having got the waist-hold from behind, place right
foot behind opponent's right heel, straighten
leg, and pull him over foot.

PLATE XLI.

THROW FROM BEHIND.

If close up to opponent, thrust right knee behind his, and throw by swinging him to right.

PLATE XLII.

THROW FROM BEHIND.

If close up to opponent and unable to place knee or foot behind his leg, slip your right foot in front of his, straighten your leg out, pulling his leg back, at the same time throwing weight forward.

PLATE XLIII.

THROW FROM BEHIND.

If opponent is breaking away from your waist-hold from behind, strike him with the sole of your right foot behind knee, at the same time giving a vigorous pull back. This will throw him backward.

Plate XLIII.

Plate XLII.

Plate XLI.

59

PLATE XLIV.

PLATE XLIV.

HALF-NELSON AND WAIST-HOLD FROM BEHIND.

Having turned opponent, slip left hand under his
left armpit and round his neck ; place right
arm round his waist, lift bodily, and throw
backwards.

Plate XLV.

COUNTER TO WAIST-HOLD FROM BEHIND
(*Position* 1).

Immediately opponent has turned and gripped you round the waist from behind, lock his arms above the elbows with your arms, crouching slightly.

Plate XLVI.

COUNTER TO WAIST-HOLD FROM BEHIND
(*Position* 2).

Bend quickly down, retaining grip, and, lifting him with your right shoulder, throw him over left shoulder.

PLATE XLVI.

PLATE XLV.

PLATE XLVII.

HAMMER LOCK AND BACK-HEEL.

Seize opponent's left wrist with right hand, thrust
it behind him and seize it with your left hand
behind his back. Now back-heel him with
your right heel, throwing your weight forward.

PLATE XLVIII.

STOP TO HAMMER LOCK.

Place your right hand under opponent's jaw and
force his head back.

65

PLATE XLIX.

FULL NELSON.

This grip, which is sometimes permitted in catch-
as-catch-can style of wrestling, is barred by
the Army Athletic Association.

66

PLATE XLIX.

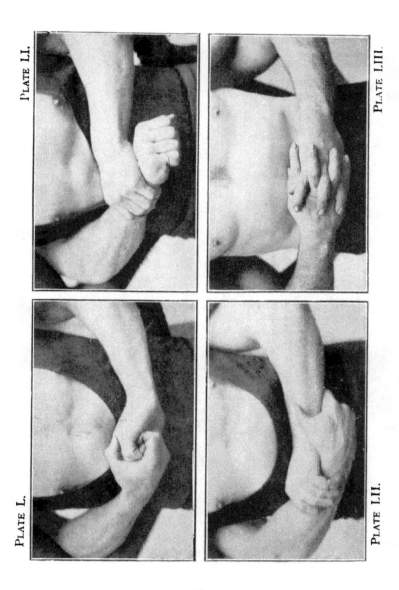

PLATE L.

PLATE LI.

PLATE LII.

PLATE LIII.

68

HAND GRIPS

PLATE L.

BUTCHER'S HOOK GRIP.

For use when arms are round opponent.

PLATE LI.

SINGLE WRIST GRIP.

For use when arms are round opponent.

PLATE LII.

DOUBLE WRIST GRIP.

For use when arms are round opponent.

PLATE LIII.

INTERLACING FINGERS.

This interlacing of fingers is not permitted.

WRESTLING EXERCISES

For the Purpose of Developing the Muscles
brought into Play by Wrestling.

Plate LIV.

FIRST LEG EXERCISE.

Stand facing each other, with hands gripped as
illustrated ; toes touching ; weight equally
balanced.

Plate LV.

SECOND LEG EXERCISE.

Lower bodies simultaneously as far as possible by
bending knees outward. Rise and repeat
according to progress.

PLATE LIV.

PLATE LV.

PLATE LVI.

PLATE LVI.

NECK EXERCISE.

Assume position shown in illustration. Lower
shoulders to mat, and resume former position
slowly. This will have a strengthening effect
in the neck and abdominal muscles.

LEG AND BACK EXERCISES.

Assume position as in illustration. Slowly straighten knees and back until an upright position is attained. Then slowly lower to ground. This will have strengthening effect on leg and back and neck muscles. The partner being raised will also obtain beneficial effect upon his abdominal and leg muscles.

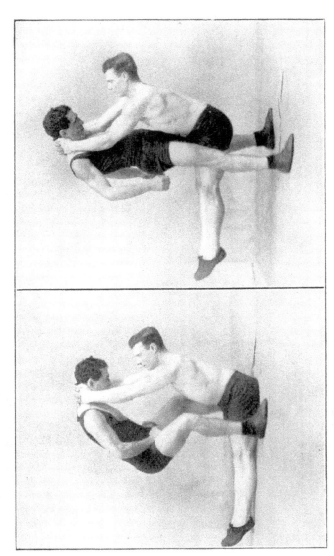

PLATE LVII.

PLATE LVIII.

PLATE LIX.

PLATE LX.

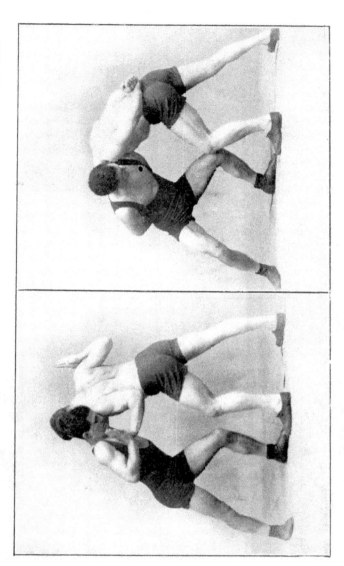

PLATE LIX.

ARM EXERCISE.

Having assumed the position illustrated, the arms are forced backwards and forwards alternately. The body should not be moved backwards. This will have a strengthening effect on the muscles of the arms and shoulders.

PLATE LX.

TRUNK AND LEG EXERCISES.

Having assumed position illustrated, gradually force weight forward and endeavour to move partner backward. This exercise will have a beneficial effect upon the trunk and leg muscles. The positions should be reversed occasionally to assure harmonious development.

PLATES LXI., LXII., AND LXIII.

SELF-DEFENCE FOR WOMEN.

Wrestling can be learned with advantage by women as a form of self-defence. Although a woman may be physically weaker than an opponent attacking her either from behind or in front, she can, if sufficiently skilled in the various throws and counters, place her assailant *hors de combat*. The accompanying illustrations show how a woman can effectively protect herself when seized in front, and how by means of the arm-throw and hip-buttock she can throw an assailant when seized from behind.

PLATE LXI. PLATE LXII. PLATE LXIII.